W9-BRO-169

BIBLIOGRAPHY
Math Fun

One for Me, One for You

by C. C. Cameron

illustrated by Grace Lin

Roaring Brook Press

Brookfield, Connecticut

Text copyright © 2003 by C. C. Cameron
Illustrations copyright © 2003 by Grace Lin

Published by Roaring Brook Press
A Division of The Millbrook Press, 2 Old New Milford Road, Brookfield, Connecticut 06804

Library of Congress Cataloging-in-Publication Data
Cameron, C. C.
One for me, one for you / by C. C. Cameron ; illustrated by Grace Lin.—1st ed.
p.   cm.
Summary: Rhyming text introduces the concepts of counting and simple arithmetic.
1. Counting—Juvenile literature. [1. Counting. 2. Arithmetic.] I. Lin, Grace, ill. II. Title.
QA113 .C34 2003
513.2'11—dc21   2002006358

ISBN 0-7613-1692-2 (trade edition)
2 4 6 8 10 9 7 5 3 1

ISBN 0-7613-2807-6 (library binding)
2 4 6 8 10 9 7 5 3 1

Manufactured in the United States of America

First edition

In thanks to God and
so many others who have shared with me
— C.C.C.

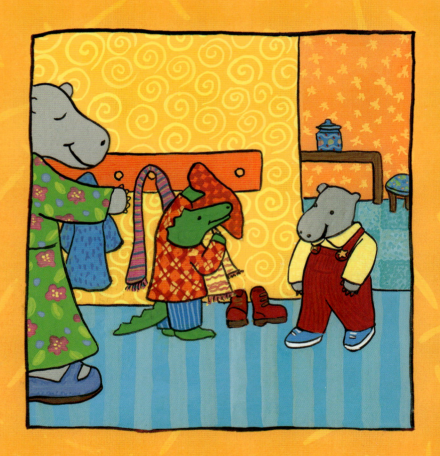

For Luke and Ranida,
and for all the cookies and cars they'll share together
— G.L.

Cookie jar.
Stool.
Cookies?
Cool!

One for me.
One for you.
That makes two.

Two for me and one for you,
or
two for you and one for me.
That makes three.

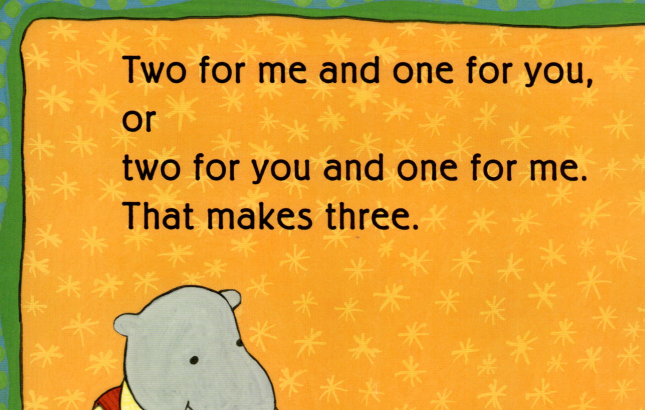

Except there's more.
We have four!

If you get three,
I get one.
(That's no fun.)

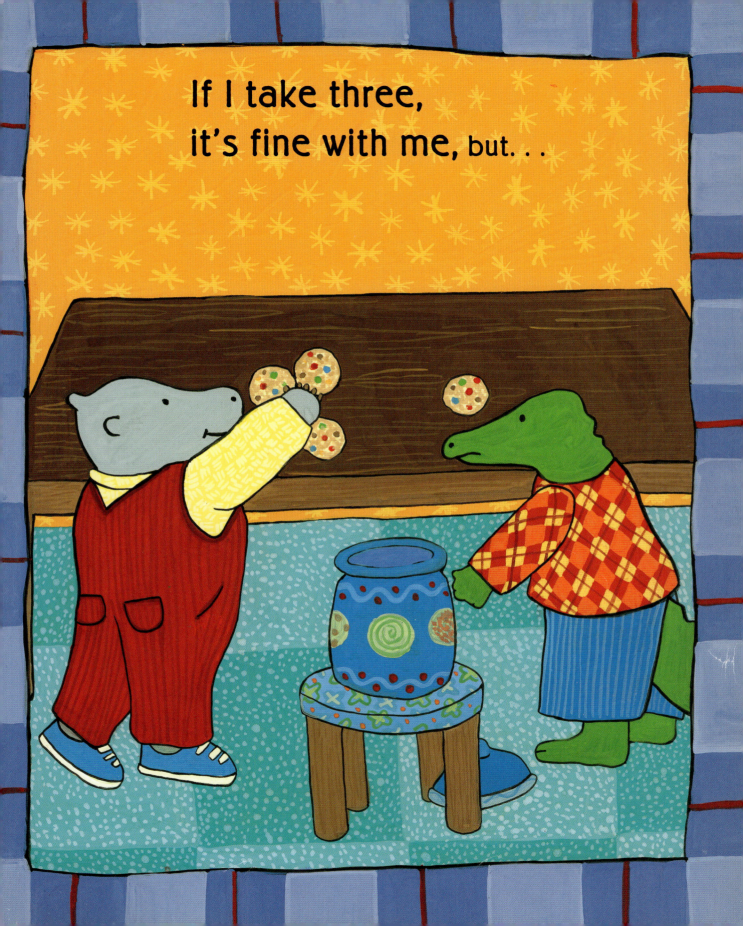

Oh. I see.
Two. Two.
It's fair. It's neat.

But please don't talk so long.
Let's eat!

Now let's play.
Cars?
Okay!

Red one, gray one, blue one—
Three.

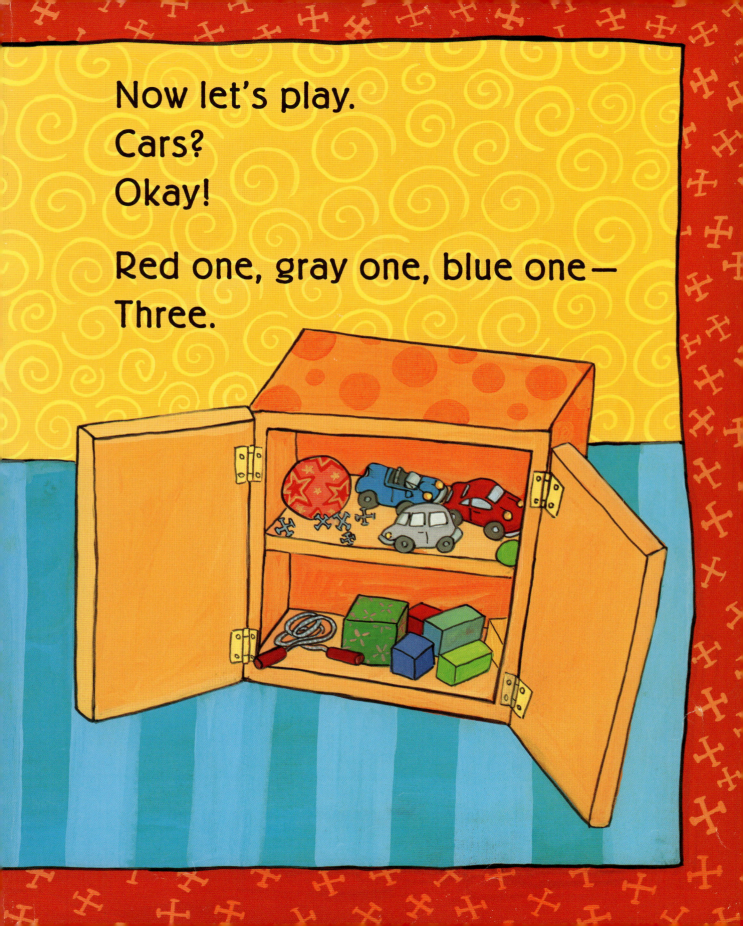

One for you.
And two for me.
Two for me is truly fine—
Two for me.
Because they're mine.

One for me?
You get the rest?
Two for you,
since you're the guest?

No! No! **No!**
Mom, see there!
She's got two,
So make her share!

Hey! Not fair!
Mom's got three!

None for you.

None for me.

So, Mom says.
Playtime ends?

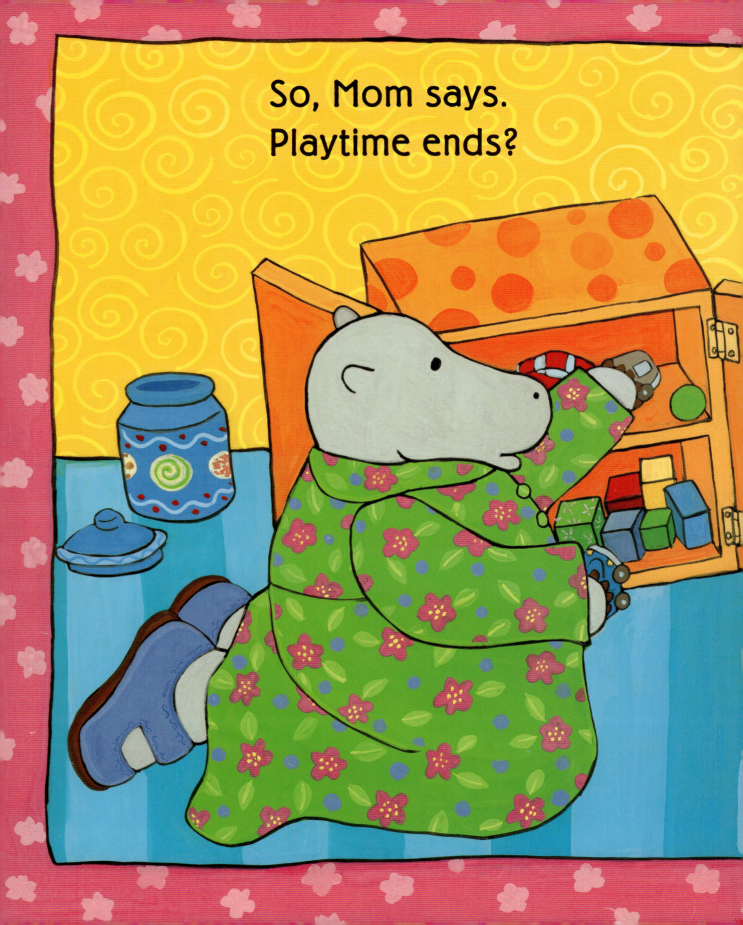

No more cookies, cars, or friends?

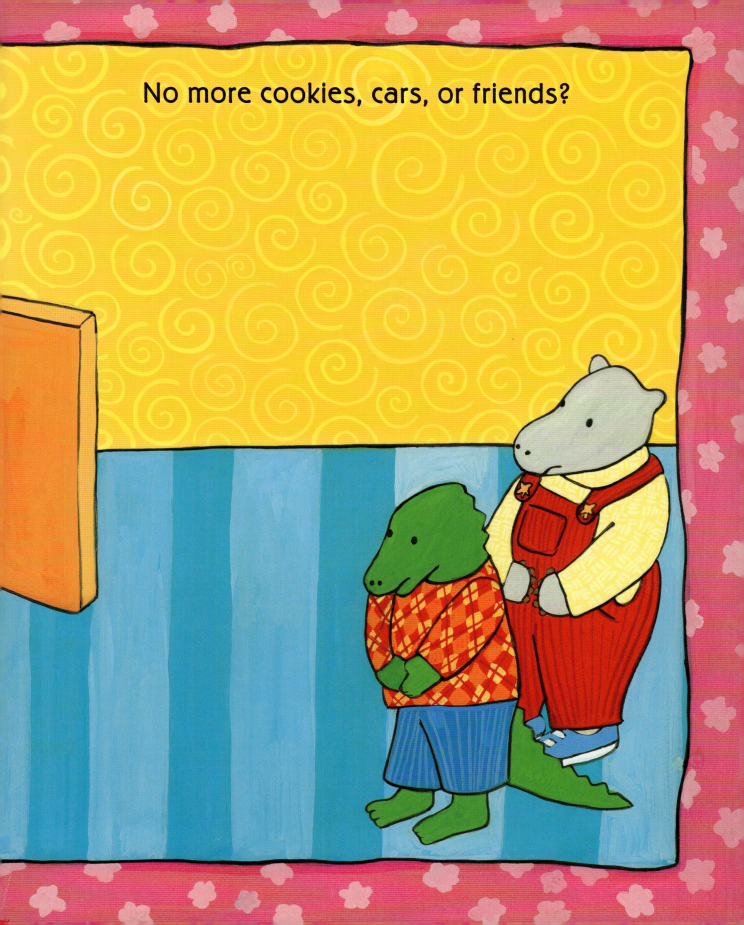

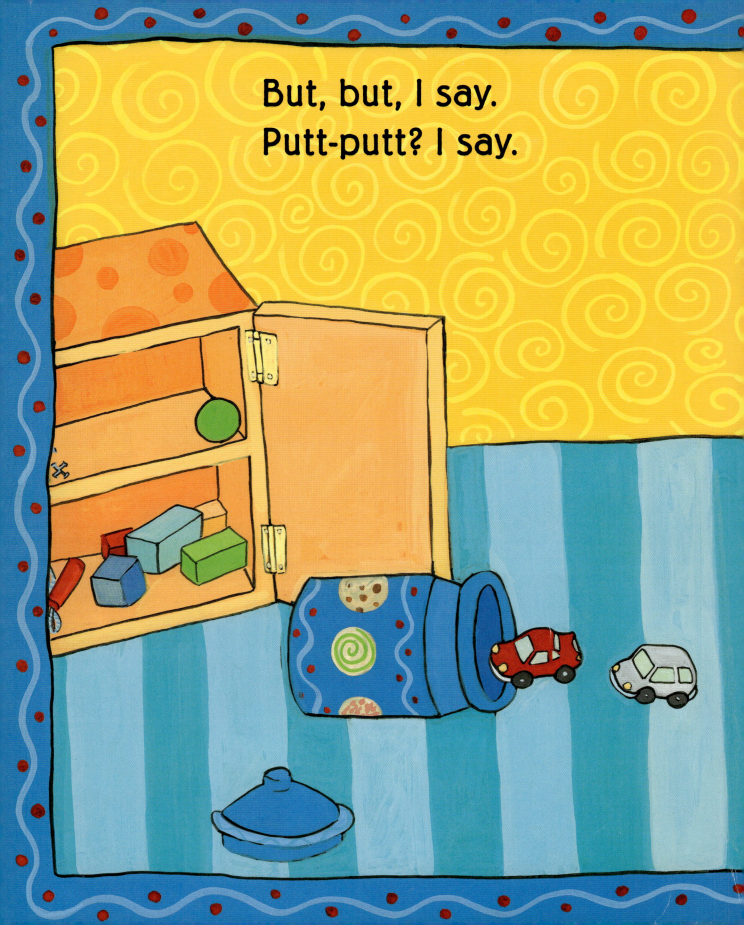

I'll run each car
Into our empty cookie jar!

Then. . .

One for you.
One for me.
One for Mom.
There! You see?

Fair for three,
and fun at last!

Catch!
Here comes the red one—
fast!